CW00832155

naming bones

joanna ingham

ignit⚡onpress

For Iris and Daniel

First published in 2019
by **ignition**press
Oxford Brookes Poetry Centre
Oxford Brookes University
OX3 0BP

© Joanna Ingham 2019

*Joanna Ingham has asserted her right to be identified as author of this work
in accordance with the Copyright, Designs & Patents Act 1988.*

*This book is sold subject to the condition that it shall not, by way of trade or otherwise,
be lent, resold, hired out or otherwise circulated without the publisher's prior consent
in any form of binding or cover other than that in which it is published and without a
similar condition including this condition being imposed on the subsequent purchaser.*

Cover design: Flora Hands, Carline Creative

A CIP record for this book is available from the British Library

ISBN 978-1-9165043-7-0

Contents

Delivering this gift
requires blood

Penelope Shuttle

Fontanelle

I want to tell you there has been a mistake.
You have left your heart too close to the surface.

It beats just under that smear of hair,
the skin's unbearable sheen.

All night it ticks, alien, molten, a stop clock
I didn't mean to set

that will go off at three with a flayed outrageous
shriek. The hospital carpark will be red soon,

raw and unlikely as a very first morning.
All the calm blue concertina curtains

can't keep me in. Your skull is the world
at the dawn of time

spinning in a ward of infant stars,
tectonic plates still shifting.

There has been a mistake. They have left
my heart in a plastic cot

for anyone to look at. It is smaller than I thought,
more helpless and more beautiful.

Visiting Gwynne

She served us tongue,
three livid discs each
on milk-blue plates.

I watched my mother
and my father
and my sister

tuck in, polite as priests.
Gwynne smiled over wet potato.
I tried not to think of

her ankles under the table,
meaty and mottled purple,
swelling her tights.

Lovely, Auntie, said my mother,
an eye on my fork,
still wavering, cold in my grip,

but my mouth was full,
suddenly, of my own tongue,
huge and full of blood

like a creature
that would live independently
if I could just cough it out.

Doing the heart in Lower Five

We try not to think of the cows, the empty churches
of their chests. Their hearts are grey now, filmed
and tubed, bigger than two fists and the air smells
like we've swallowed money, like we've licked
the edge of a knife. My partner retreats to the sickroom
so I probe alone, fingers where the blood should be,
aorta a handless glove. The valves are bell tents
like Christian Union camp in the RE teacher's garden,
each ventricle a mouth that opens again and again
when I squeeze it, the preacher from St Matthew's
telling us he can help us speak in tongues. It's heavy,
this meat, this site of love we haven't felt yet
and I wonder if the cow did, if the beating quickened
for the bull, for the wet slicked nose of its calf.
The notes in my drawing are neat – mitral, tricuspid,
inferior venal cava – as if I'm striking a bargain
with knowledge, like the words will keep me safe.
Then it's break and we can wash our hands, drop
our hearts in a bucket like the babies in the abortion
video they made us watch, let the portacabin,
its swollen walls, pump us out into the light.

That night

the house was strange with you in it,
and me strange too.

You wouldn't let me put you down
and I was crazy with missing my own arms,

the ease of filling the kettle with two hands,
of pulling up my trousers.

We read that babies like the warmth of bodies,
the smell of someone they love already,

so your dad took off his jumper, soft
and kindled from his chest,

and laid it in your basket
that we called your Moses basket without question.

I was frightened but I tried to sing the songs
I thought I had forgotten,

put you down as slowly as a bomb disposal expert,
leaving my hands on you until the last moment

then edging away, turning down the volume
on the Darts World Cup by one number every minute,

dimming the lights like stars going out very slowly
near dawn, willing you to go on sleeping

without the sound of my heart, this first night
of our long parting.

Flight

They've fitted me a black box in my chest,
here, wired into the sinews. It's recording
all the time, even now as I type, because
you can never be too careful. My laptop
exploded once and there are viruses, fatal,
with names like ILOVEYOU. It records
while I sleep because cancer can start in
the dark, blossoms open like a greedy star.
Crossing roads, it ticks, vigilant. It's set
for motorway driving, clifftop roads that
snake, greasy and chancy, through the fog.
Even hot chocolate with marshmallows
can be risky, even my own tongue, which
it's possible to choke on. It's actually orange,
my black box, emergency tangerine with
an underwater locator beacon and cockpit
voice recorder so you can hear me screaming
help, please help me, oh god no – fireproof,
shockproof, waterproof, they'll always find it.
If you put your hand against my heart, you
might be able to feel it, the hard edge of it,
there under the fragile perilous sheer of my
skin. And if you think you can hurt me any
more, you can't, because my black box sees
it all, keeps it safe for a future time when
they will learn what you did, every human
error, electrical fault, short circuit, every
thing we could have stopped but didn't,
every point on our map where there might
have been a different outcome, destination,
where people lived and went home to their
families, weeping with relief in airport lounges,
and the fuselage stayed intact and wasn't
floating in the middle of the Atlantic Ocean,
and teams of divers didn't have to go searching
for the pieces that are left of us, the box
that still pings for you six thousand metres down.

Welney

The morning after the swans
it snows. I watch you
in the half light,
still sleeping under down
as flakes scud against the window –

think of the swans last night
creaking in off the fens,
a stream of heavy white
above us,

their necks in the floodlights
as they fed,
loops of throat
and muscle,

and you beside me
as the swans went on calling over,
their wings changing the air
like you,
like snow.

At the Bernina

after Tony Tost

It's easier if you have someone who knows what they're doing
to show you. Otherwise the pattern lifts and twists, you cut off
the little triangles that were meant to guide you, and Simplicity
is anything but.

                        The zipper tries to knit but the foot is wrong.
The gathers snag and the binding shifts from the lip of the armhole,
which gapes. The machine eats the threads, but secretly, under the linen,
so you don't see until it's too late and you end up cutting yourself
on the anxious smile of the unpicker, and you swear inappropriately and
rip the seams you've already stitched, which were looking quite good.

I don't know how to talk about my mother so I will talk about a dress.

It fits but you can't see that.
It becomes an apology in Liberty print.
It would suit you if you'd let it.

Autumn, East London

He brings me seventeen apples from the garden,
green and crisp in his arms.
Smell one, he says, and it smells of grass in the country in summer.
We stand there for longer than we need to,
his arms full of apples – *seventeen!* –
and wonder where they came from,
this bounty, unlooked for and undeserved,
these green suns, these bee dreams,
these gifts of trust, clean rain.

Neutrogena Norwegian Formula

And though I resent it some nights
when I am tired and leave my clothes
in a heap so I can get into bed quicker
and put out the lights as a hint,
though I complain it's vain, this method
I can see even in the dark, how precisely
you place each pea-sized squeeze
on each knuckle and work from wrist
to tip, unhurried even when I tut,
quite unlike my own slapdash approach
of squirting a big gob and rubbing at it
blindly, and only then if I've noticed
my palms are stiff from a walk in the cold,
though I am jealous, even, of the attention,
your thumbs in their fastidious circles,
the way you knit your fingers, ease
each cuticle, and feel driven to question
whether sailors in Norway with hands
far larger than your small to medium
would spend half as long on their
personal grooming, and even when
I say, *do you have to do that now,*
can't you just live a little, leave it, risk it?
I am grateful. Let me say this here
if nowhere else: I forgive you.
Meticulous man, I have watched you
at your rituals twenty years. Those hands,
unremarkable but for their softness,
that have painted this duck egg room,
planted me daffodils and jasmine,
carried me tea every morning, turned
my pages in the bath, cupped a frog,
made me come, over and over,
held our daughter that first time like a god.

Geckos

You tell me that I slept all night
under the fan's broken heartbeat
as geckos, translucent, curious, naked,
came and went through holes in the walls
on quiet sucking feet.
All night, you didn't touch me.
It was too hot, you say.
This morning we stand on cracked tiles,
bucket water over each other.
You tell me how you stood by the window,
saw, through the wire grill,
a black and white moonscape
of elephants herded round the jeeps,
a river of shadow-dark deer
and monkeys, poised silver in the teak.
You wash the sweat and dust from my scalp
and I wish you had woken me.
I accuse you of dreaming,
that this was a night safari of your own making.
I do not tell you
I wish you had touched me anyway,
let me climb into your sleep,
let the deer flow through us on their silky hooves.
This morning geckos hide under the room's skin.
The fan rocks loose in its socket.

Choughs

Ours is the only tent,
angled to catch the nuclear
glow from Wylfa.

It is already September.
The wind guffaws across
the Irish Sea.

Unzipping the morning
we find seven choughs
blacker than space.

They dig for leatherjackets,
worms, in the flat places
bared by campers.

Lifting, they shred the air,
flash red scimitar beaks,
electric cries.

He wraps himself around me
in his sleeping bag like a grub.
They nest in sea caves,

he says. The choughs dive
over the wide cliffs, shrugged
against the cold.

Strannik

> For all its reputation, the pike is the most delicate of all
> the freshwater fishes, just as Rasputin was but a man.
> John Andrews in On Nature

At Bosherston one suspends itself
in yellow shadows – muscular, bearded,
conjured from a branch.

Nothing moves. The lilies are enamel.
Lust stuns the pike into a long stillness,
a summer topaz longing.

It will be there too as ice heals like skin
over the ponds, makes a winter palace,
a depth of mysterious gifts.

Kneel down. You must let the pike
recover briefly in the sack. Unhook it
and cock the jaw open.

Do not shoot it at close quarters,
do not beat it in the eye with your boot,
do not tip it back through a hole

in the ice on the Malaya Nevka River
in December, its beaver hide coat
belling it to the surface.

Hold the fish by the root.
Hold it steady in the shallows.

The Paedophile

My sister's piano teacher threw
himself off the Orwell Bridge.

I pictured his yellow teeth
pierce the surface of the water,

saw him caught under struts
by shopping trolleys, rocks,

his fingers still playing scales
in the fishy grey current.

How strange that one week a man
can sit in a cheap white shirt

on one of your dining room chairs
watching your sister's

untalented hands crouch over the keys,
and the next be bobbing

face down under the road your father
takes home from the office.

Threw himself, that's what they said,
but I wonder if he only dropped

like rain from a cloud, an apple from
a tree, the way he had to.

Skeletons

He liked to test me
on the names of bones –
clavicle, phalanges –
till I foundered
and he could rescue me,
enunciating them, one by one,
in his textbook tongue.

I thought it was for me,
this trying to catch me out,
me with my A in Biology.
Later he stopped naming bones
and I saw it was for him,
this wanting to show
he had saved these words
like scalpels and lint, like men
still strapped in their planes.

He used to laugh sometimes
about the chap in two bits,
flung from the cockpit, guts
wrapped around a tree,
and how they unwound him,
tried to put him back together.

The optician's assistant

It's astronomy, he says.
My eye is a planet

newly captured on his screen,
orange, floating, crazed,

the image beamed from
light years away, a wonder

of science. We discover it
together. *That's the optic nerve*,

he points, *the macula lutea*.
I watch him map ancient rivers,

what might be a mountain range,
a mysterious plain. His eyes

are brown, fine lashed and very close.
There is only the machine

he uses to puff air at me
between us. Once a doctor

told me my cervix was perfect,
a perfect rose.

At Felixstowe

I could have been loved by a fish shop boy,
sixteen, acne urgent as a flare.

But I was going to university.
Thought I had taste, laughed in his face.

I think of him now in the queue for cod
and chips as another boy dips

a battered slick into the trembling fryer,
how I could have unwrapped him

by the bins, his pickled egg white skin,
the hair still soft on his lip.

You might think you got away

that your blood isn't pink, thick with flossed sugar from the stall
by the arcades, that your eyes aren't fringed by coloured bulbs
in scallops, that cranes don't light the dock of your heart. You
might say it wasn't you on stage at the Spa Pavilion dancing to
'Chariots of Fire' in a green leotard, or eating cake at The Regal
after.

You're not the kind of person to work for two pounds an hour
in a shop called Serendipity selling *The Star* and gobstoppers and
rock, the word Felixstowe in its marrow, with a girl called
Donna, her postcard tits. Or the kind of person to pick up fifty
quid dropped by a coach-trip pensioner blowing down the prom
and go halves with the boy you snogged under the war memorial
because you didn't know you could say no yet.

You can pretend you can't remember crazy golf, the plastic lion,
its hungry mouth, or the machine they had at the leisure centre
to make safe blue waves with no shit in them, or the men fishing
off the end of the pier as if they thought they could reel in jobs
or women, or the Mannings girls, the fairground daughters,
hair blonde as California, or the way your daddy smelt after
snooker, like salt and grey, or the other boy, the one you loved,
waltzing you round the community hall in the stiff prow of his
arm without looking at you once, or your nana's swimming cap,
its rubber blossom bobbing between the tankers.

On Ramsey

She wades after the warden, still unsteady,
knee-deep in heather and thrift. He has a trick
to show her, a Manxie's voice on a pocket recorder.
They kneel at the cupped mouth of a burrow,
play the calls, a male high and rasping,
the female's answering growl.
The girl leans closer.
Her ear is trained to the chance of a bird,
the secret underground, a crouch of grey feathers.

The Corpse Road

Six men take the corpse road to St Oswald's.
The seventh, stiff, waits on a coffin stone
as they eat their lunch, watch the sleet blossom.
The dead are heavy. Years they should have lived
pile up in them like boulders, weigh them down.
Today, the wind from the mere is grey with ice
and moss clings hard to the trees. The men drink
to the man in the box, colder than they are.

One, the youngest, pulls a lock of fleece
from the dried spikes of a teasel, thinks of
a girl he tries to please, her hair like this,
pungent and coarse in his fists. On the road,
his shoulder under his father, the boy
sees her winter eyes, her summer body.

What autumn is for

We choose our leaves –
you, a yellow beech still veined with green,
me, sycamore, its heart a flame-splayed star.

Dusk is falling and across the park
lights blink from the cafe, bikes thread
their paths through the trees.

You hold up a leaf, oak this time,
half crumbled already, your small hands
eager as you push it towards me.

I offer cherry, tooth-edged, curled,
but cool and smooth with dew.
You nod and we stow our finds like misers.

So we make our slow meandering way,
bag rustling against the buggy, weightless
with gold. You point out the moon,

that new thing, and frown to check I am looking.
I had not known hours could pass
in the patterns of leaves. I had not thought

I could surrender myself to this quiet,
feet buried in a drift of brown,
these hours. *Here*, I say, triumphant

as I lift a leaf, the bones of a leaf,
red-purple lace fine enough
to breathe through.

Acknowledgements

Many thanks to the editors of the following publications in which versions of these poems have appeared: *Ambit*, *The Best British Poetry 2012* (Salt), *The Fenland Reed*, *Magma*, *The North*, *The Sunday Times*, *Under the Radar* and *BBC Wildlife*.

Epigraph is taken from Penelope Shuttle, 'Giving Birth', in *The Lion from Rio* (Oxford University Press, 1986).

My gratitude also goes to Arvon, the Poetry School, Liz Berry, Sarah Dickenson, Suzannah Evans, Sarah Hesketh, Alice Hiller, Lisa Kiew, Kathy Pimlott, Jacob Polley, Kate Potts, Richard Price, Jean Sprackland, Anne Stockley, Liane Strauss, Natalie Whittaker, my family and friends.

Thank you to everyone at **ignition**press.

FSC
www.fsc.org

MIX

Paper from
responsible sources

FSC® C015185